THE QUICK EXPERT'S GUIDE TO

Starting your own business

Adam Sutherland

WAYLAND

First published in 2012 by Wayland

Copyright © Wayland 2012

Wayland
338 Euston Road
London NW1 3BH

Wayland Australia
Level 17/207 Kent Street
Sydney, NSW 2000

Senior editor: Julia Adams
Design: Rocket Design (East Anglia) Ltd
All images and graphic elements: Shutterstock

British Library Cataloguing in Publication Data
Sutherland, Adam.
   Starting your own business. -- (Quick expert's guide)
   1. New business enterprises--Juvenile literature.
   I. Title II. Series
   658.1'1-dc23

ISBN 978 0 7502 7048 9

Printed in China

Wayland is a division of Hachette Children's Books,
an Hachette UK company

www.hachette.co.uk

>>>CONTENTS<<<

TO THE UTTERLY EXCELLENT WORLD OF BUSINESS!

Congratulations! If you're reading this book, you're on the right track to becoming an entrepreneur. This is someone who chooses to take matters into their own hands, and goes into business for themselves. You could be making cupcakes for a local tea shop, or importing vintage Ferraris from Italy — if you're standing on your own two feet and running a business, you're an entrepreneur.

Starting your own business can be one of the most exciting — and scariest — things you will ever do! You can experience the thrill of putting your ideas into practice, and acting on your own initiative.

At the same time, you need to plan very carefully to ensure you get off to a good start and, just as importantly, be prepared to react to customer feedback and constant changes in the market if you are going to make it to the top and stay there.

PLACE YOUR FEET IN THE STARTING BLOCKS AND GET READY FOR THE QUICK EXPERT TEAM'S DEFINITIVE HEAD-START TO SUCCESS!

Get tips **straight** from the multi-millionaires' mouths...

...who started a business in their **teens.**

Follow our step-by-step **guide** to writing an outsanding business plan.

Understand how to reach a **global** market.

Get tips on coming up with an **original** name for your company.

Find out how to survive the **ups** and **downs** of running a business.

Chapter 1

HAVE YOU GOT WHAT IT TAKES?

Ask anyone who's done it and they'll tell you that starting your own business is one of the most rewarding — and challenging — times of their life. And while we can't guarantee you success, we can help you plan, organise and manage your business as carefully and efficiently as possible to give it the best chance of not only surviving, but thriving.

✳ FIVE REASONS TO START A BUSINESS

1 ✳ ### You can be your own boss (for once)

At school and at home, you've got teachers and parents telling you what to do and when to do it. Starting your own business will give you the freedom to do things your way, and put your own ideas into practice. Be warned, though, you still have to answer to your customers if you don't get things done when you say you will!

You can do something that interests you

2

The best thing about being an entrepreneur is that you can choose what sort of business you want to start. You might have a passion for selling old teapots online, or running fitness classes for your friends after school. Whatever it is, you can turn a hobby into a profit. Which brings us to...

You can make some money

3

We often read about entrepreneurs like Mark Zuckerberg, who started **Facebook** in his university bedroom and is now worth billions! Don't expect to be buying your own island straight away, but with hard work and the right idea, you could certainly be giving your pocket money a much-needed boost.

You can be creative

4

Being creative doesn't just mean being good at drawing or making things. It can mean creative thinking — dreaming up good ideas that will help your business to grow, and then seeing them through. The most successful entrepreneurs are always thinking of new ways to improve their business and make it stand out from the crowd.

You can turn your dreams into reality

5

You're probably not thinking any further than making some extra cash, and enjoying the chance to express yourself and make your own decisions. However, it is possible to make it really big — just look at UK businesswoman Martha Lane Fox, who became a millionaire thanks to her entrepreneurial achievements.

Martha started an online travel and gift business called **Lastminute.com** in 1998 and two years later it was **'floated'** on the stock market. The company was valued at a whopping £733m, and Martha made £13.5m from her shares. The sky's the limit if you work hard!

meaning people were able to buy shares in it

✳ WHAT'S THE RIGHT BUSINESS FOR YOU?

You've been inspired by our five reasons to start a business, and want to have a go for yourself. Congratulations! Now it's time to really get your thinking cap on. Choosing the right business, and having a clear idea of what your business does (and — just as importantly — doesn't do) are going to be vital to making your business a success.

Base it on a skill or interest

If you're going to put in the amount of time and effort required to make your business a success, make sure you choose something you actually like doing! It could be baking cupcakes, mowing lawns or making balloon animals at children's parties — if the business goes well, you'll be doing a lot of it. If you don't enjoy it, it will be even harder work.

Write a list of what you're looking for from your ideal business

For example, it will need to fit around the school day, and can't cost loads of money to set up. If you're good with computers, you might consider learning how to build and design websites. **Google** founders Larry Page and Sergey Brin came up with their idea for Google search while they were students at Stanford University. The computer code that made them both billionaires cost nothing more than their time to write it, and was actually produced for a college project! Plus, the Quick Experts Team have an excellent book on how to build a website, so you're halfway there already!

❋ Research the competition

Looking at the most successful businesses locally and nationally in your field of interest will give you some really useful tips from people who are doing it right. It might also make you adapt your own idea slightly so you don't put yourself in direct competition with an already strong and successful business. If you can't do it better or cheaper, the best advice is to think about trying something entirely different.

If you're planning to open an eBay shop, for example, then the concept of local competition doesn't apply, but you should still investigate who is selling the same sort of goods that you plan to sell, and research their prices, stock and **sales methods**. ←

for example, do they offer 'buy one, get one free' or a 'buy now' option at a discount?

REALITY CHECK

OFFICIAL REALITY CHECKER

THIS CARD CERTIFIES THAT
_ _ _ Melvin _ _ _
IS OFFICIALLY CERTIFIED TO CHECK REALITY ON BEHALF OF THE QUICK EXPERTS GUIDE

APPROVED

☑ Facebook fame

Harvard University student Mark Zuckerberg didn't like to take no for an answer. His previous school had run an online list of students – a 'Facebook' – and Mark wanted to know why Harvard didn't have the same thing.

When he was told that the university believed it affected students' privacy, and didn't support the idea, Mark decided to ignore his tutors and build it himself.

Mark's Facebook launched at Harvard in 2004, expanding firstly to other prestigious 'Ivy League' universities in the USA, then high schools, businesses and eventually worldwide. If Mark had done what he was told, the online world would be a very different place!

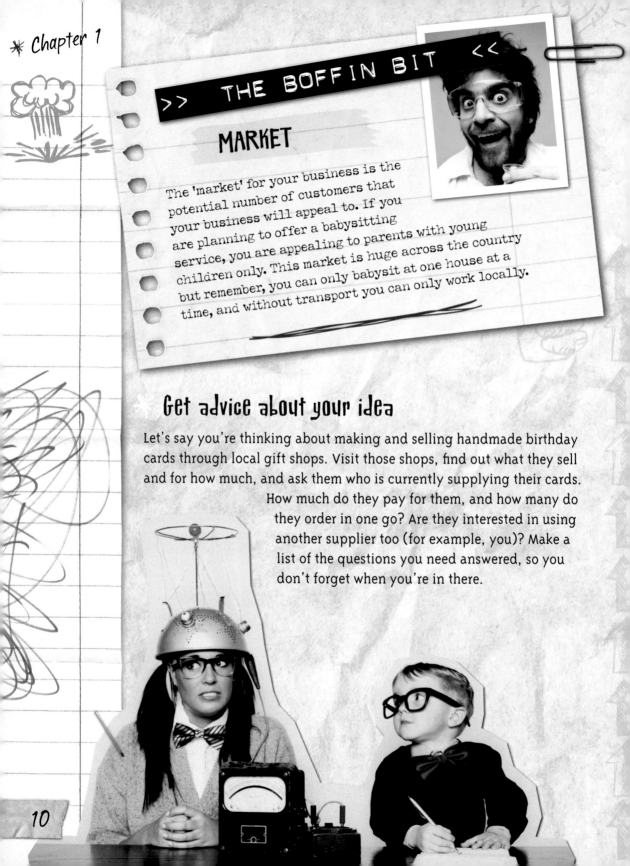

MARKET

The 'market' for your business is the potential number of customers that your business will appeal to. If you are planning to offer a babysitting service, you are appealing to parents with young children only. This market is huge across the country but remember, you can only babysit at one house at a time, and without transport you can only work locally.

※ Get advice about your idea

Let's say you're thinking about making and selling handmade birthday cards through local gift shops. Visit those shops, find out what they sell and for how much, and ask them who is currently supplying their cards. How much do they pay for them, and how many do they order in one go? Are they interested in using another supplier too (for example, you)? Make a list of the questions you need answered, so you don't forget when you're in there.

Decide if you need any money to start, and if so how much

Most businesses need a little money to start with. If you're making cakes, you'll need ingredients, and possibly even a mixer. If you're going to offer maths tuition to younger students, you'll need your bus fare to your students' houses and maybe some textbooks. Plan ahead and work out how much or how little you need. And be honest with yourself. Mum and dad might be happy buying the odd bag of flour, or giving you a few lifts. But every day? If your business gets busy, you'll soon have to stand on your own two feet.

DIY DUDE Entrepreneur's Checklist

Complete our checklist to find out whether you're ready to be a successful entrepreneur:

1. Are you positive, optimistic and enthusiastic? (Do you always look on the bright side?)

2. Are you creative? (Do you enjoy dreaming up new ideas?)

3. Are you outgoing and confident? (Can you talk to people you have never met before?)

4. Are you decisive? (Can you make a decision and stick to it, even if others don't agree with you?)

5. Are you a good communicator? (Can you explain things to other people so they understand them?)

6. Are you self motivated and hard working? (Are you prepared to get stuck in and work long hours to achieve your goals?)

Mostly Yes: Congratulations, you definitely have what it takes to make it as an entrepreneur!

Mostly No: Starting your own business is hard work, and you're not quite there yet. But keep working on some of the characteristics above, and you'll be an entrepreur in no time!

Dude!

11

✳ TEN QUESTIONS TO ASK YOURSELF BEFORE YOU START

So we've inspired you to start a business, and you think you've got a great business idea. Now ask yourself these ten tough questions to help you decide if you're really onto a winner.

✳ Is it Coke or Pepsi?

Your business doesn't have to be original. After all, **Pepsi** launched to take advantage of the market that **Coca-Cola** had created. But you do need to establish a few **unique selling points** if you want people to buy your product or use your service instead of a competitor's. Are your cupcakes organic? Do you include house-cleaning with your babysitting service?

USPs for short

✳ Do people want it?

Before you do anything else, make sure you thoroughly research the market for your new business. Are there enough people out there who would use it or buy it? Customer demand is what will support your business and help it grow.

✳ What's your business model?

In other words, how much will you charge people, and what will you be charging them for? If you're starting a business building websites for local businesses, think of additional ways you could make money. Could you expand to national and international companies, for example? If there are other businesses out there doing what you're doing, look closely at how they run their business and learn from it.

✳ Is the price right?

It's no good having the best product or service on the market if no one can afford it! On the other hand, you need to make sure that you can receive some reward for the time and effort you'll be putting in. Talk to potential customers about your pricing to see what they think, and what they would be prepared to pay.

4

✳ What will stop others from copying you?

You hear it all the time on Dragons' Den — what's going to stop another bigger company coming along and stealing your idea? Strong USPs (like great customer service) can help here.

5

✳ Do you know your customer?

Build a profile of your target customer. Is it young mums? Pensioners? Learn whatever you can about them, seek them out, and take every opportunity to listen to what they have to say. What do they value most in a product or service like yours?

6

✳ Can you make a profit?

How much does it actually cost to produce your idea? If you're baking cakes, or building websites, take into account what you have to buy to be able to create your product or service. If you need to spend £200 on computer software to start designing websites, how many websites will you have to work on to pay back those costs?

7

8 ➤

✳ Do you have enough money to get started?

You might be in the fortunate position of not needing any money to get started. After all, you're not renting an office or hiring five members of staff. But if you get an order for two dozen cupcakes with vanilla icing and silver sprinkles, can you afford the ingredients to make them? It's sensible to put some **money aside** to cover these early set-up costs, before money starts coming in.

called a 'cash reserve'

9 ➤

Do you have the skills, experience and ambition to pull it off?

Remember, even if you have the best idea in the world, it won't work without the drive, passion and commitment to see it through. Will you stick with it when the going gets tough? If not, you'll be an also-ran instead of a front runner.

10 ➤

✳ Can the business grow?

It might seem a long way off, but it's worth thinking about how you can expand your idea in the future. Maybe opening a shop, renting office space, offering other services. With any luck, this could be a business that's making you money for many years to come!

SAY WHAT?

❝ *When we start a new [business], we base it on hard research and analysis. Typically, we review the industry and put ourselves in our customer's shoes to see what we could do better.* ❞

Sir Richard Branson,
Chairman of Virgin Group

BE A QUICK EXPERT!

Research your potential market before starting your business.
Ask yourself questions such as:

- Do people want what you plan to offer? If not, why not?

- If there is a demand, can you put a financial figure on it? (In other words, how much money do you estimate it can bring in per week or per month?)

- What other companies are offering a similar service or product?

- How successful are they?

- Can you improve on what they're offering, or make your business different enough from what they do?

Chapter 2

LAYING
THE FOUNDATIONS

No new business is a guaranteed winner, but you can drastically increase your chances of succeeding by putting maximum time and effort into the early stages. Not only will it help you anticipate and prepare for potential problems, it will also give you a clear direction to pursue.

* KNOW YOUR MARKET

First things first. No business can succeed without providing goods or a service that customers want. But how do you find out what people want? By asking them! This is called market research, and experts believe that well-targeted market research is the number one difference between your business succeeding or failing.

Finding out about your market should start before your business is even launched. You need to know a) is there a demand for the business you're planning to launch, b) is someone already doing it, and if so c) is there room for your business too?

* Hit the high street

If you're hoping to supply a product or service to other local businesses — maybe selling ornaments or greetings cards — visit local shop owners and ask them, 'Would you buy from me?' Don't be upset if you get some 'No's. The most important thing is to get useful feedback on what businesses want and don't want from suppliers that could save you several months of trial and error.

You can also use your high street trips to investigate businesses that are offering similar products or service as you. You might find that a lot of companies are already working in the area of business that you have targeted. Think carefully: this could mean there's strong demand. In which case, great! It could also mean that you will face fierce competition. Not so great.

If competition is strong, you will need to think of a plan to make your business stand out. Whether it's offering the lowest prices, promising fastest delivery, or something else entirely, you need to think of something that will give your business an edge.

✳ Look online

The internet is a quick and simple way of testing the demand for your business. You can do this by first of all making a list of keywords that people would type into a search engine if they were looking for a company that provides the same product or service as you. For example, for a dog walking business you might include the keywords 'dog walking', 'dog walker', 'dog exercise' and your postcode/town. Remember to make a note of these keywords for when you want to **launch your own website**. ⟵

See page 41

Any internet search will quickly list all the companies that you will be competing with if you launch. If there aren't any: well, you've obviously hit on an original idea. But is there a market for it? If there are lots of companies: you know there's a demand, but is there room for you? Assess the competition, find out what they're offering and decide if you can improve on it. What are their strengths and weaknesses? Do they have a good reputation? The more you know, the better equipped you will be.

✳ Try it for yourself

Depending on what kind of business you're hoping to launch, your next step for market research is to check out the opposition first hand — either yourself, or with the help of friends and family. There's no better way of finding out the quality of the competition and how successful they are than by sampling it for yourself. So eat their cakes, ask them to walk your dog, get them to wash your car.

Find your rival's **unique selling point**, and decide if you can match it. Do your market research well enough and you will be able to organise your business in a way that will give you a real head start.

Dude!

DIY DUDE

Practise your business skills

Practise your business skills by choosing a range of new businesses – from babysitting to homemade soup deliveries – and researching what exists in your area.

Now take a sheet of paper and fold it lengthways down the middle. On the left-hand side write down the competition's USPs. On the right-hand side write down what you could you do better, cheaper, faster and so on. For example, if you were researching pizza deliveries, companies often compete on speed of deliveries, and prices/special offers (eg buy one, get one free). This exercise will get you thinking about competition, and what you can offer to make your business unique. It will also help you to complete our SWOT analysis at the back of the book.

✳ PUTTING YOUR THOUGHTS ON PAPER

The next step in creating a successful business is to write a business plan. Even if you're only planning something small that you can do at the weekends to make a few extra pounds, a business plan will help you set targets, plan for the future and, just as importantly, confirm to you that your idea is realistic and can work!

Over the next few pages we will explain what a business plan should include, how to go about writing one, and what you'll achieve by doing it. Pens and paper at the ready...

✳ Why you need a business plan

It puts all your ideas and research into one place — not on scraps of paper on your bedroom floor!

A business plan helps you decide if the business can work.

With the help of a plan, you can set out the strategy for your business, including how you will make people aware that it exists.

Your business plan will set targets and objectives, including sales targets, so you can keep an eye on the performance of your business.

✳ What should be in it?

Every business plan is different, but the headings below are useful guides and will make sure you tackle the most important points

Contents
At the start of your business plan, list the main sections and page numbers. That way, you and anyone else reading it will be able to find all the important stuff quickly. We're listing it first because it will go at the start of your business plan, but you will probably want to write it last, when you know your plan's entire contents.

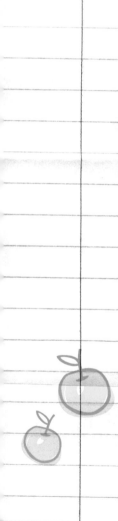

Summary

This is your business chopped down into just a few sentences. In it, you explain:

- Your name and address, and details of the business

- Details of the product or service you plan to sell, for example: "I plan to offer a Cookie A Day service. People pay £5 per week and get four fresh cookies delivered to their door every morning".

- A summary of your target market, for example "School children who want cookies for their lunchbox; dads who want them for an afternoon snack; mums who want them for the journey home from work", and the competition you think you will face.

- What makes your idea, service or product unique or original, and gives you an edge over the competition.

Aims and objectives

Here's where you explain why you want to start this particular business and what excites you about it. Think about questions like: Why are you going into business, and what do you want to get out of it? A new XBox, maybe? Or to save money toward driving lessons when you turn 17? Also think about whether you plan to work on the business for years to come or is it just for one summer holiday? Will you be able to run the business on your own, or will other family members or friends be helping you?

The answers to these questions will have an effect on the way you run your business, and the plans you make. For example, if you're only doing this to earn money for an XBox, you will probably want to aim for a business you can start quickly, and end just as quickly. Washing your neighbours' cars or babysitting for their children would be cheaper and less time-consuming to organise than, say, advertising as a children's entertainer for birthday parties, which would require practice and quite a lot of equipment.

Business description and purpose

What will your business actually do? Be as specific as possible here about the type of business you want to start. If you're going to make gifts for local shops, for example, explain what sort of gifts they will be. Will you be making earrings and bracelets? Designing greetings cards? Knitting scarves and gloves?

In what way will your product or service be different from what's already on offer? Why would customers come to you, and not someone else? Try to make your description straightforward. It needs to be so simple, even Mum and Dad can understand it!

Marketing strategy

To make your business a success you need to know your target market — from school children to pensioners. How big is the market, and what share of it can you hope to sell to? Car washing is a good example here — every house on your road is a potential customer (as long as they have a car), but some of them like to wash their own cars, some get their own children to do it for pocket money, and so on. Your target market can sometimes be smaller than you first think.

Think about the following:

- Who is your target market?

- What special deals can you offer them to try your product or service?

- What is your USP and how does this make you different from your competitors? For example, you make the only 30-centimetre chocolate chip cookies on the market!

Marketing plan

Once you have a marketing strategy, your marketing plan will explain how you will achieve your objectives. It will include:

- The marketing methods you will use. Maybe you will design leaflets or business cards to advertise your business, for example.

21

- How you will reach your audience. You might put your cards through people's letterboxes, or put leaflets on the notice boards in local shops.

- The cost of your marketing. Bear in mind the costs of paper and photocopying here.

- How you will react to any responses you get. If you are offering a 'same day service' for ironing shirts, for example, could you manage to do that if 20 people placed orders at the same time?

>> THE BOFFIN BIT <<

PROFIT AND LOSS

A profit and loss statement is a company's financial report that indicates how the **revenue** (money received from the sale of products and services before **expenses** are taken out) is transformed into the **net income** (the result after all revenues and expenses have been accounted for).

It shows the revenues for a **specific period,** and the cost and expenses charged against those revenues. The purpose of the profit and loss statement is to show the reader quickly and simply whether the company made or lost money during a certain period.

usually a year

Sales targets

Your marketing plan is then converted into something very important — your sales revenue target. In other words, how much money you think you will make! The figures you put in here will mostly be guesswork, but try to estimate in terms of sales by amount and by value (for example selling 50 cupcakes at £1 each comes to £50) and sales to different customer groups (for example schoolchildren, adults).

Financial forecast

Don't get scared here. This doesn't need to be too complicated, but you should include **any money you have to spend** to start the business, and any money you will need from week to week to keep the business running (for example more cooking ingredients for your cupcakes, bus fare to deliver ironing to customers' houses and so on).

costs of leaflets, car washing equipment, and so on

From this you can produce something called a Profit and Loss forecast, which is really just a sum:

Money that you have made from sales − Costs (things you have had to buy)
= Profit (or Loss!)

Keep this sum in your head, and however complicated it seems, you shouldn't get too nervous about the finances.

> ❝ We see our customers as invited guests to a party, and we are the hosts. It's our job every day to make every important aspect of the customer experience a little bit better. ❞
>
> *Jeff Bezos, founder and president of Amazon.com*

SAY WHAT?

SWOT analysis

This isn't a list of teachers' pets, it stands for **S**trengths, **W**eaknesses, **O**pportunities and **T**hreats, and it helps you focus on the strengths and weaknesses of the product or service you plan to offer, and get an all-round view of the future of your business.

On pages 60-61, we have included a sample SWOT grid. Take a copy of it and fill it out with your own business idea. Make sure you answer all the difficult questions. The more truthful you are, the better prepared you will be, and the more chance there is that your business will be a success!

A healthy SWOT analysis will include more 'Strengths' than 'Weaknesses'. But don't worry if you can list a few 'Threats', just as long as you can think of ways to overcome them.

✳ MISSION STATEMENT: YOUR BUSINESS IN A NUTSHELL

A good mission statement will explain your business in less than 30 seconds. That makes it one of the most important, but also trickiest, parts of your business plan! Your mission statements should answer these questions:

- Why does the business exist?
- What is your unique selling proposition?
- What are you committed to providing to your customers?
- What promises are you making to your clients?
- What wants, needs, desires or problems does your product or service solve?

An example of a bad mission statement

'To deliver high profits to shareholders through providing a broad range of services to customers, thereby enhancing their ability to succeed.'

What does this company do? What do they care about? Why should we buy from them?

Examples of good mission statements:

REALITY CHECK

OFFICIAL REALITY CHECKER

THIS CARD CERTIFIES THAT
_ _ _ Melvin _ _ _
IS OFFICIALLY CERTIFIED TO CHECK REALITY ON BEHALF OF THE QUICK EXPERTS GUIDE

APPROVED

☑ Furniture mogul

Sarah Green started earning her own money at just 12 years old by delivering newspapers. It was on her paper round one day that she realised lots of old age pensioners' gardens were in need of attention. So she designed a flyer on her computer offering a garden tidying service, put them through letterboxes on her paper round and within a fortnight, she had eight customers, and was earning £40–50 per week!

By the time she was 18, Sarah had started an online furniture company, www.1st-for-furniture.co.uk, which made more than £400,000 of sales in just its second year of trading. Sarah currently has three employees and her own fleet of vans to make home deliveries.

Tips for writing a great mission statement

Don't do it on your own.
Even if you're running the business by yourself, it will help to get at least one other person's ideas. Someone not involved with the business will find it easier to see strengths and weaknesses that you might miss. Think about asking friends or family for their advice; as long as you are confident they will take it seriously!

Set aside plenty of time to work on it.
Mission statements are short — sometimes as little as one sentence. That doesn't mean writing one will be quick, though! It takes time to come up with the right words and language to not only describe your company, but to inspire you every time you read it.

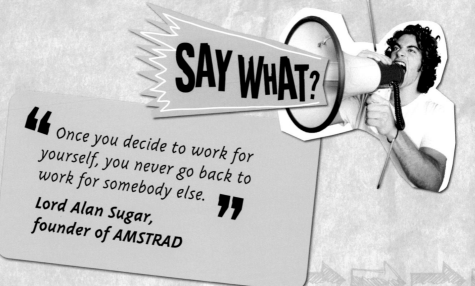

SAY WHAT?

" Once you decide to work for yourself, you never go back to work for somebody else. "

**Lord Alan Sugar,
founder of AMSTRAD**

Plan it carefully.
Write a list of topics to think about. Find a quiet place away from TV and other interruptions and start scribbling.

Be prepared.
If you have several people involved, have drinks and snacks at the ready, as well as plenty of paper and pencils. Because not everyone will understand what a mission statement is, you might have to explain its meaning and purpose before you begin.

Brainstorm.
Consider every idea, no matter how silly it sounds. Look at other companies' mission statements for inspiration. If you're working with friends, try to find a large flip chart to write down ideas so that everyone can see them. Once you've finished brainstorming, ask everyone to write individual mission statements for your business. If necessary, you can pick the best bits from each, and fit them together!

BE A QUICK EXPERT!

- Research the market.

- Learn about your competition – what they're doing right, and what they're doing wrong. It will help you see gaps in the market.

- Prepare a business plan.

- Following the structure and discipline of a business plan will get your thoughts in order, generate ideas and help you focus clearly on your business' strengths and weaknesses.

READY TO START!

You've asked yourself the right questions, written your business plan and now you're ready to start. In this chapter, we will explain the practicalities of starting your own business: from choosing what sort of business you should be (yes, there is more than one type!) to legally setting up and registering a company name. You might be tempted to get started straight away and worry about these questions later, but our advice is to take some time and get the legal side of your business right from the beginning. It could avoid lots of problems later.

What sort of company should I be?

There are three types of company:

- Limited company
- Partnership
- Sole trader

There are advantages and disadvantages to each type of business, but we are going to focus here on sole trader. It's the most advisable way to start your first business, as long as you plan it properly and get a grown-up's advice where necessary.

What does sole trader mean?

Sole trader means when one person is the owner of a company and has complete control over it. That person is you! Sole trading businesses are usually small — often with no employees apart from the owner — but there are loads of them. In fact, the 2.3 million sole traders in the UK make up over 70 per cent of British businesses.

REALITY CHECK

☑ Scooter millionaire

Dominic McVey, 27, became a millionaire at 15 by importing micro-scooters. "At about eight, I went to Japan with my dad, who was a percussionist with the Royal Shakespeare Company, and brought back a load of gadgets. I sold them to my friends for a 20 per cent profit. At 13, I was looking for Visa on Yahoo! but spelt it wrongly and discovered Viza, a 'push-scooter' company based in Arizona. The man I contacted there said: 'Buy five and I'll give you one for free.' I sold 11 million scooters; I used to send a container a week to Japan."

Dominic was inquisitive and always disguised his age, doing all his business on the internet from his bedroom. "Whenever I did meet companies, even if I thought I couldn't get any business out of them, I asked them a million and one questions about how they did business. They loved telling me because they felt like the older brother telling the kid what to do."

OFFICIAL FORM C-185A

✳ Why choose sole trader status?

Sole trading businesses are popular because they are simple and fast to set up. You don't even need a separate bank account for your business (although you will need to keep records of what is personal spending, and what money is coming and going from your business). If your business thrives and becomes bigger, you can always become a limited company or partnership at a later date. Your bank will be able to explain all the legal requirements to you when or if that time comes.

Depending on how much money your business makes, you might be liable to pay tax. For full details on this, talk to your bank, or ask your mum and dad to speak to an accountant.

SAY WHAT?

❝ *'You've got to love what you do to really make things happen.* ❞

Philip Green, British businessman worth £3.3bn, whose family own Topshop, Topman and Miss Selfridge

✳ What should I call myself?

Whether you want to call yourself The Ace Cookie Company, or Jack Jones' Carwash, there are legal rules about choosing a company name. First of all, if you want to use something different from your own name, you will have to produce company letterhead with the company's name and address on it. Whenever you send a letter or give someone a bill, you should use this letterhead. Luckily this doesn't need to cost you anything other than an hour fiddling about on your computer with some fonts!

As a sole trader, you are not legally required to register your company name, but we recommend it. You can do this online with the **National Business Register**. Certain words like 'international' or 'federation' are restricted, and you are also not allowed to use the same or a similar name to an already existing business as it could cause confusion, and get you in trouble with the original owner. So you can't call yourself McDonald's Hamburgers — even if your surname is McDonald!

There's more advice on choosing a name in the next chapter (see p. 34).

http://www.start.biz/home.htm

We have come up with five different types of businesses:

✳ **Homemade pizza delivery**

✳ **Milkshake bar for teens**

✳ **Mobile carwash service**

✳ **Dog walker**

✳ **One-on-one help for exam preparation**

Using the advice from earlier, come up with three good names for each business, and three bad names! What makes one name good and another one bad? What do they tell you about the business, or make you think about when you hear them? Get your thinking caps on!

DIY DUDE

Get a good name!

Dude!

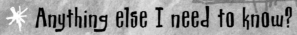 Anything else I need to know?

Depending on what sort of business you are planning to run, you should check with your local council if you need a trading licence. The government has also passed certain laws that you need to make sure you don't break! These include:

⦿ The Trade Descriptions Act

You can't claim that the earrings you make are made of gold if they're not, or that you only use organic ingredients in your cakes if you don't.

⦿ The Sale of Goods Act

Everything you sell must be good quality and as you describe it. Twelve-inch cookies need to be 30 centimetres not 15 centimetres, for example.

⦿ The Supply of Goods and Services Act

You have to take reasonable time and care to carry out the service that you are offering — however much homework you still have to finish!

This isn't a complete list, but it gives you a good idea that what you are planning to do is important and should be given your full time and attention.

GET REAL!

Andres Cardona launched a basketball club in Miami when he was just 14. He wanted the club to be a place where neighbourhood children could get together, learn skills, get fit and have fun. The club is free, but Andres makes money from events and tournaments that he arranges.

"I'm doing this for the local community and for kids my age. I created the sort of club that I wanted to join.' A bigger, competing club tried to buy out Andres but he refused. 'I don't want to give this up. I love it!"

Search for South Miami Basketball Academy on Facebook

E-TRADING

With the growth of the internet, and particularly websites like eBay, there has been a massive growth in people called e-traders. An e-trader is someone who either sells things online they have made themselves, or buys goods and resells them online.

If e-trading is going to be your business, you should still follow the instructions above regarding setting up your business and registering a company name. HMRC, the government department responsible for collecting taxes, has employees who regularly check auction websites for busy traders, so watch out!

Her Majesty's Revenue and Customs

BE A QUICK EXPERT!

- Choose a type of company that suits you – we recommend sole trader status because it's quick, easy and cheap to get started.

- Register your company name – be careful not to choose anything that's already taken by a business doing a similar job to you.

- Be aware of trading laws – if you're providing goods or a service, you are subject to certain government rules and regulations.

CREATING A BRAND

You've already put a lot of thought into your business and now you're finally ready to get started! But how do you attract customers, and start making money?

A big part of your business will be making your product or service stand out from the competition, and trying to attract new customers. In other words, creating a brand! There are several ways you can do this — from learning and fulfilling your customers' needs on a regular basis, to building a great website. First of all, we're going to return to something we mentioned in the last chapter: the importance of your company name.

✳ WHAT'S IN A NAME?

Your company name is usually the first thing that any potential customer will come across, so it's as important as your sales pitch and even your end-product! You could have the best idea or product in the world, but if your customers are going elsewhere because the competition looks and sounds better, you will never get your business off the ground.

The company name is the entry point to your business — like it or not, customers make judgements on what products they want to buy and where from based on a name. You do it yourself. Think about your favourite clothes or foods; would you buy a packet of Boggs Biscuits, or a jumper from Rubbish Clothing?

When you're choosing a business name, remember: it's something that you will have to say hundreds of times every day, and it's something that (hopefully) will become well known. Be 100 per cent sure you like how it sounds, and how it looks when it's written down before making your final decision.

It might be tempting to include your own name into your business name — after all, you will see hundreds of small businesses like this, from John's Joinery to Trish's Tea Shop, but does it add any information about your business? The answer is no. The ideal name should be original, clever and instantly explain what your business does.

There are three types of business name:

- **Descriptive** — these describe what the business does, or are named after the owner. For example, **BetFred**, **Lastminute.com** or **Comparethemarket.com**.

  Pros: Provides information about the company, or who runs it.

  Cons: Not very exciting, and can be less memorable when you are starting out.

- **Associative** — these try to create a positive association, or link, in customers' minds. For example, **In Trim Hair Salon**, **Touch of Class Dry Cleaning** or **Speedy Car Hire**.

  Pros: Helps to generate a positive company image.

  Cons: If you're not careful, they can sound cheesy!

- **Abstract** — these may have no meaning at all, and can just be words joined together. For example, **Pinkberry** (frozen yoghurt), **Gap** (clothing) or **Dune** (shoes).

  Pros: Can attract attention, and are usually original.

  Cons: Provides no information about your company and what it does.

When you are choosing a business name, make sure:

👁 It's not already taken.

👁 It doesn't have any negative meanings — not just in English, but in other languages too!

👁 It reflects what your business stands for.

👁 It's easy to say — and spell!

👁 It's easy to remember.

👁 It can be registered as a URL or web address

👁 It won't limit the growth of your business (for example, naming your business after the town you live in, may make it difficult to grow to other areas).

👁 You should also carry out an internet search on the name to make sure nothing negative comes up associated with the name or words you are planning to use.

Some of our favourites...

BATTERSEA CODS HOME

(fish and chip shop)

TREE WISE MEN

(tree surgeons)

SARNIE SCHWARZENEGGER'S

(sandwich shop)

SELLFRIDGES

(second-hand fridges)

ONLY FOODS AND SAUCES

(takeaway)

ABRA- KEBAB-RA

(kebab shop)

DUSTIN OFTEN

(house cleaners)

...and they are all real!

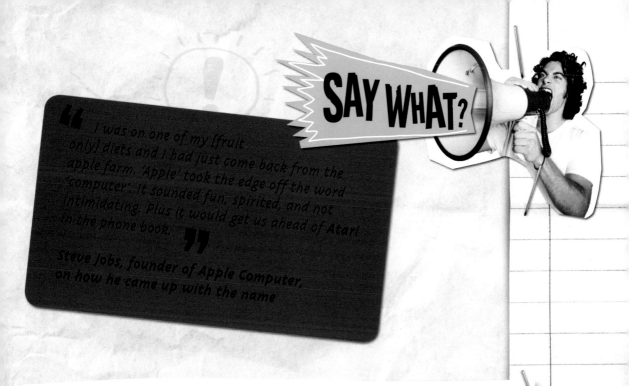

SAY WHAT?

> " *I was on one of my [fruit only] diets and I had just come back from the apple farm. 'Apple' took the edge off the word 'computer'. It sounded fun, spirited, and not intimidating. Plus it would get us ahead of Atari in the phone book.* "
>
> Steve Jobs, founder of Apple Computer, on how he came up with the name

✳ BRANDING YOUR BUSINESS

Successsful companies don't just have clever names, they develop great brands. A brand is not just your company name or the font you write it with. Put simply, your brand is your promise to your customer. It tells them what they can expect from your product or service, and it differentiates your business from your competitors.

Your 'brand' is made up of who you are, who you want to be, and how people think about your business. You can be cheap, fast, reliable or health-conscious — just as long as you have something about your business that helps people remember you.

Building a strong brand will help customers choose you over a competitor because they will feel they know what they are going to get from your product or service — even before they buy it.

Brands are built on three rules:

Confidence — you will win the confidence of your customers by doing exactly what you say you will do. For example, 'Next Day Shirt Ironing' really needs to happen within 24 hours.

Emotion — brands like **Apple**, and certain clothing companies make their customers feel good. Think of the emotion you feel when you buy a new iPod, or put on a new pair of trainers. Brands attract customers by creating a unique personality for their business.

Consistency — this is the hardest part. What it means is retaining your customers' confidence, and delivering an emotional response to your product… over and over again. A brand builds over time, and you have to always keep your standards high. In the restaurant business, they say 'You're only as good as your last meal'. Try to remember that!

>> THE BOFFIN BIT <<

BRANDING

All the qualities and features of a product, including its name and its appearance, are presented to the customer as a brand. To be successful, all brands – from **Facebook** to **McDonald's** to **Nike** – need to be distinctive (stand out in some way from competitors), consistent (always provide the same level of quality, and therefore be seen as reliable), recognisable (through a logo or 'look' of a product) and attractive. The blue Facebook logo, for example, has become as recognisable as a Nike swoosh or the McDonald's golden arches.

DEFINING YOUR BRAND

Deciding what your brand stands for can be time-consuming and difficult. Some companies take years and spend thousands of pounds researching it. Luckily, we're going to save you time and money by suggesting that you answer the questions below:

- What are your company's goals?

- What are the benefits and features of your product or service?

- What do your customers already think of you or your company?

- What qualities do you want them to associate with your company?

Once you've defined your brand, how do you get the word out? Here are a few simple, tested tips:

Get a great logo. And make sure you place it everywhere.

Memorise your brand message. What are the key messages you want to communicate about your brand? For example, 'We're the fastest/cheapest in town.' Remember them and use them!

Be the brand. Branding extends to every part of your business: how you answer your phone, what you wear to meet customers, your email signature, everything.

Create a catchphrase. Write a short, memorable statement that captures the essence of your brand. For example, Apple uses 'Think different'.

Be consistent. Use the same colour scheme, font and logo on any printed material your company produces. You don't need to be a design genius, just consistent.

Be reliable. Customers won't return to you — or recommend you to their friends — if you don't deliver on your brand promise.

Still used by many US taxi companies today!

REALITY CHECK

OFFICIAL REALITY CHECKER

THIS CARD CERTIFIES THAT

_ _ _ Melvin _ _ _

IS OFFICIALLY CERTIFIED TO CHECK REALITY ON BEHALF OF THE QUICK EXPERTS GUIDE

APPROVED

☑ Twitterpreneur

As a child, Twitter founder Jack Dorsey was fascinated with street maps, and how taxis found their way around busy cities. In his teens he wrote a computer programme that directed taxis to customers needing a ride.

While working at software company **Odeo**, Jack suggested a new programme to his bosses that would use a form of text messaging so people could let friends know where they were. Odeo executives came up with the working title of twttr – inspired by the photosharing website **Flickr** – before later rebranding the company as **Twitter**, and adding the distinctive 'Larry the bird' logo. "We came across the word 'twitter', and it was just perfect," Jack remembers. "The definition was 'a short burst of inconsequential information', and 'chirps from birds'. And that's exactly what the product was."

Jack himself sent the first message on 21 March 2006. By the end of 2012, Twitter had 140 million active users, sending 340 million tweets per day!

the message read:
'Just setting up my twttr'

OFFICIAL FORM C-185A

✳ GOING ONLINE

As more and more people surf the web to research companies they want to buy from, the name (known as 'domain name') that you register for your website is becoming just as important as your main company name.

Depending on the product or service you plan to launch, a website could be a vital part of your marketing strategy. We'd need a whole separate book on building a website (in fact, we've done one) so here we'll just focus on the importance of choosing and registering your domain name.

Why? Because a well-chosen domain name such as **www.childrensparties.com** or **www.homemadecookies.com**, could mean that instead of going in search of your customers, they will be contacting you!

But you don't always need a name that explains exactly what you do. Take **Amazon.com** — the name says nothing about the books, DVDs and clothing they sell. But just as importantly, it is short, memorable and helps the company stand out from the crowd.

Choosing a domain name

Stuck for ideas? Use **RAIL!**

Recall — Is your name easy to remember?

Aesthetics — How does it look when it's written down?

Impressions — First impressions are very important. Aim for a positive response

Length — A short name is better than a long one!

Your name can contain numbers, letters and hyphens, so don't despair if **www.johnscakes.com** isn't free, try **www.johns-cakes.com** instead, or even a range of other domain endings, from .co.uk, .net, .org and so on. .Com is still the best known domain ending, but .co.uk tells people you're a British company, which might be important depending on your business.

How to register your domain name

It's easiest to register your domain through an internet service provider (ISP). Some examples are **123-reg.co.uk, godaddy.com** and **fasthosts.co.uk**, but there are literally hundreds of others. For a fee of around £10 per domain name per year, the ISP will do all the necessary work behind the scenes to make sure the domain is live within a couple of days.

The world's most expensive domain names

Companies can pay millions of pounds for extremely popular domain names. Here are a few examples:

www.poker.com (£12.4m)

www.beer.com (£4.3m)

www.pizza.com (£1.6m)

www.cruises.co.uk (£560,000)

www.recycle.co.uk (£150,000)

www.mobile.co.uk (120,000)

Of course, you don't need to spend a fortune to create a strong, memorable brand. Some brain power, research and hard work will do the trick just as well!

DIY DUDE

Get a good name!

* Visit the websites of five brands that you use every day.

* List five things that their websites do well, and five things that they do badly. Explain your answers too.

* Remember these good and bad points when you are ready to build your own site!

Dude!

BE A QUICK EXPERT!

* Choose a company name that's easy to say and remember. Ideally it should also describe what you do quickly and clearly.

* Make sure that someone else isn't already using it, and that the web address is available.

* Decide the key values of your brand – is it price? Fast delivery? Friendly customer service? Make sure that everything you do reflects these values.

TELLING the WORLD

You've researched the market, written a business plan, and launched your business! You're sure there are hundreds of people out there who want what you're selling. But how do you let them know about it?

Business people use the term 'marketing', which just means how you present your business to customers, and how you let them know about it. Try and put yourself in your customers' place: if they wanted a new website built or their grass cutting, how would they find out about your business?

Established businesses can spend a lot of money on marketing. Here are our top tips for marketing your new business virtually for free:

✳ HIT THE STREETS

If you're offering something that would particularly appeal to people in your neighbourhood, go door to door putting leaflets or business cards through people's letterboxes. Be clear about what you're offering, and how you can be contacted. If possible, even include a price.

GRASS CUTTING
and general garden maintenance
Prices from £5 per hour
References available
Contact Toby on 07744 5647566

✳ TELL A FRIEND

Businesses talk about the value of 'word of mouth'. That means one customer recommending you to another potential customer. This is the best way of expanding your business, as people trust recommendations from friends, and often act on them.

So how can you get your customers to recommend you? One great way to get people to pass on your details is to offer discounts — perhaps 10—20 per cent — to every existing customer who passes your details on. When new people get in touch, you should always ask, "How did you hear about us?" That way you'll know what's working. And just as importantly, what isn't.

>> THE BOFFIN BIT <<

VIRAL MARKETING

Viral marketing uses social networks like **YouTube, Twitter** and **Facebook** to present a message, which is then spread by word of mouth with one person telling another, in a similar way that a virus or disease spreads through the population. A good example of this was a **Cadbury's** TV advert of a **gorilla playing drums** to a song by Phil Collins. Because the ad was unexpected, funny and memorable, it got people talking about it, emailing the link to their friends, and spreading it around the world more than any traditional advertising campaign could ever have hoped to do!

type Cadbury Gorilla into YouTube to see it

※ WORK YOUR CONTACTS

When you start a new business, you will need customers fast. Think about all the people you know, and all the people they know. Who would be interested in the product or service that you're offering? Write a short explanation of your business and email it to everyone you know. Remember to reply to everyone who responds, and to keep them up to date with your progress. That way, you're building strong customer relationships.

※ WEAR OUT YOUR SHOES

Once you've worked out who your potential customers are, go where the business is. In other words, go to places where these customers shop, eat, drink, relax and either talk to them personally or try to put leaflets or flyers on the notice boards of these places.

※ EMPLOY MUM AND DAD

If you're offering a shirt ironing service, for example, get mum and dad to put up a sign at their offices. You're targeting business people here — so the more office workers who know about your business, the better!

REALITY CHECK

☑ Super successful

At 19 years old, Julian Dunkerton opened a market stall in Cheltenham in 1985 under the name **Cult Clothing**. Over the next 15 years, he grew it into a nationwide chain with an annual turnover of £17m.

In 2003, Julian launched a new fashion brand, **Superdry**, with two friends, and they opened their first store in London's Covent Garden. They had no money to spend on advertising or celebrity endorsement, but one of the company's leather jackets was photographed on footballer David Beckham. This 'celebrity endorsement' proved to be the ultimate advertising tool! The jacket sold 70,000 units and became the company's bestseller.

The cult of Superdry was born, and since 2008 the brand has expanded worldwide and is now sold in over 20 countries on four continents. In 2010, Superdry was floated on the London Stock Exchange and Dunkerton is believed to be worth £180m!

Wow, serious money!

OFFICIAL FORM C-185A

* TEN IDEAS TO MAKE YOUR BUSINESS MEMORABLE

1. **Offer free workshops** for young children about your product or service. This could be great if you make greetings cards, or bake your own cupcakes. The hints and tips you give don't need to be complicated, they just need to get people interested.

2. **Record a video** talking about an aspect of your business, or even better demonstrating something you make or do. When it's done, upload it to **YouTube** and email the link to anyone you think would find it useful.

3. **Write an article** explaining one of your specific skills. If you organise children's parties, it could even be a few jokes! Then post it on your website, blog, and other other similar websites. We all know more about something than someone else does, so promote yourself as an expert!

4. **Write a press release** about your business and send it to your local newspaper.

5. **Give a speech** for careers day at a local school.

6. **Create a customer loyalty programme**. For example, 'Get your grass cut twice, and the third time is free!'

7. **Design a monthly newsletter** on your computer and email it to all your contacts.

8. **Read your local newspaper** and look out for new businesses opening in your area. Send them a brochure, a business card and whatever your latest promotion is.

9. **Team up with a non-competing business** to offer a promotional package. If you make cupcakes, a local café would be a great partner.

10. **Start a 'Customer of the Month' competition**, where each month you highlight one customer who uses your product or service on a regular basis. Make sure you advertise this online, in local shops and so on.

Choose a typical business that a teen might start – for example, making and selling cupcakes. Think about what challenges will face your business (competition from supermarkets, people choosing other kinds of cakes or snacks) and how you might tackle them. Also think about the future of your business. What things might happen six months, a year or even two years from now that might affect what you're doing (for example, a new cake shop opening on the high street, less time to bake because of exams and so on). These questions also relate to the SWOT analysis you'll be completing at the end of the book.

DIY DUDE

Think about it!

Dude!

BE A QUICK EXPERT!

- Network – talk about your business to family, friends, and anyone you think will want to use it.

- Be visible – try and become known for your skills, experience or the service you are providing. Use the internet to spread the word, if possible.

Chapter 6

HOW TO GET MONEY AND HOW TO KEEP IT!

If you want to make your business a success, you will need to sell what you do. You might not consider yourself a natural salesperson, but if you have had the determination and ambition to start your business from scratch, you are almost certainly the best person to sell it to customers. Follow these simple steps, and you will be making sales in no time!

✳ DRAW UP A SALES PLAN

Your sales plan is simply a list of potential customers. In other words, people you think will buy from you. Don't include mum and dad, grandma, your little sister — however tempting it is. You need to think about next-door neighbours, school friends, parents of school friends, local businesses... The list will be different depending on what product or service you are offering.

✳ WRITE A PITCH

Your sales 'pitch' is an explanation of why someone should buy from you. It's what you use when you speak to every potential new customer — either face to face, over the phone, or even by email. Write down some brief points about the product or service you offer, how it can benefit customers, and what sets you apart from the competition. Look back at your list of points, pick the 3-4 best ones and then write them into a paragraph. Try out your sales pitch on friends, relatives, anyone who will listen. Get their honest opinion, rewrite your pitch, and keep working on it until it's right. Your sales pitch is the key that will unlock customers' wallets.

✳ MAKE CONTACT

Some people don't mind **'cold calling'**. If this isn't for you, try sending introductory emails, explaining who you are and a little bit about your business, and then following up on the phone. When you ring, you can start by asking, 'Did you receive my recent email about...?'

picking up the phone and ringing complete strangers to pitch their business

✳ FINDING THE RIGHT PERSON

If you are selling to a large company, chances are there will be someone between you and the person you need to speak to. This might be a receptionist or a **PA** who has instructions not to put sales calls through. If this is the case, introduce yourself, be polite and friendly, but be persistent. It might take a few calls, but with luck you'll eventually get to speak to the person you need.

personal assistant

✳ TAKE A DEEP BREATH...

However nervous you feel, try to speak slowly and calmly, make regular eye contact, and prepare to answer questions when you finish. The fact is, sometimes you will get a 'No'. When this happens, try to find out the reasons why — it might help you improve your presentation, or even your product. If you get a 'Yes', congratulations!

✳ THE IMPORTANCE OF GETTING PAID

A sale is not a sale until it has been paid for. Therefore it's crucial if your business is going to prosper that you make credit control a priority. Credit control is how businesses describe the discipline of making sure they get paid promptly.

'Credit' means offering your product or service without being paid for it straight away. A window cleaner might wash your windows while everyone is out at work or school, for example, and come back a few days later to get paid. This is offering credit.

If you're making birthday cards for a local gift shop, they may ask to pay you after the cards have sold. You don't have much choice in this, but consider asking for some money upfront to cover the cost of your card and other materials, and agree a payment schedule with them for the rest of the money. Can they pay you for sales after two weeks? A month? Try and make a deal that works for both of you.

Offering credit to a customer should be a calculated risk, but never a gamble. You can get basic training in credit control from the → **Better Payment Practice Group** (BPPG).

Other ways to get paid on time:

- ◉ **Send out an invoice** with payment terms clearly stated

- ◉ Make sure your invoices are **sent as soon as the job is done**, or your product has been delivered

- ◉ **Keep your paperwork filed** so that you know what is owed by whom, and for how long

- ◉ **Make a timetable** for chasing payments — starting with the oldest first

www.payontime.co.uk

✳ BALANCING THE BOOKS

For lots of grown-ups, one of the scariest things about starting a new business is handling the accounts. So we don't expect you to feel any differently. But don't ignore it! If there's anything you don't understand, ask an adult for advice.

see page 28

If you're setting up as a **sole trader**, then your bookkeeping will be pretty simple. You will have to keep track of your **monthly income** and expenditure (money going out to pay for things like cake ingredients or leaflets to advertise your business). And keep hold of all your receipts!

payments coming in from sales

You could manage your accounts on paper, but it's easier to use a computer. Set up a simple spreadsheet with columns for invoice and expenditure and keep it up to date. That means you will need to keep a record of **all the invoices you send out**, and all the receipts for work-related purchases (see above). It shouldn't take you more than a couple of hours every month.

including the dates they were sent, and the dates they were paid

If you become liable to pay tax, this is all the information you will need to be able to fill out a tax form. But again, if you're in any doubt, talk to an adult.

GET REAL!

At 15, Jess Ratcliffe came up with the idea for GaBoom, an online video games swapping and sales service. Although her business sadly closed in July 2012, the experience has not put Jess off.

"[If you think you've got a good idea, my advice is] just go for it! It's such a great learning experience and the fact that you have the power to turn your idea into reality is fantastic. I would also say trust your gut instinct at all times."

gaboomswap.com

DIY DUDE

Designer dude!

Design a sample invoice, which you can send out to customers every time you finish a job and want to get paid. Try and put yourself in the customer's shoes – what information do they need to know to be able to pay you?

Make sure it includes your business name, address, email address and contact number. Think how you will make it look: where will you put the company name and logo?

The customer you are sending it to might receive 100 invoices a day, so make sure you clearly explain what it is you are invoicing for (a unique job reference number is useful here), when the job took place and so on.

And how do you get paid? Your bank account details need to be on there – either the name of your bank account for cheques, or the name, account number and sort code for bank transfers.

Dude!

BE A QUICK EXPERT!

🔵 **Sales – be prepared**
Write a 'pitch' (an explanation of why someone should buy from you) and practise it on your friends and family until you know it by heart. Then use it!

🔵 **Get paid**
Design an invoice including all the relevant details (your company details, job you are invoicing for, amount and so on), send it promptly, and chase it if necessary.

🔵 **Keep accurate records**
Make sure you know what jobs you have done, what dates you did them on, how much you have invoiced for, and which invoices have been paid (and, just as importantly, which ones haven't!)

Chapter 7

IMPROVING AND GROWING

* MANAGING YOUR TIME

Congratulations, your business is a success and you're busy, busy, busy. In fact, too busy! If you're not sure how you can achieve everything you need to achieve with just one pair of hands and 24 hours in a day (and homework to do too!) then read our top tips for managing your time effectively.

- **Carry a notebook** and write down everything you do, think about, and talk about for a whole week. This will help you understand how much you can get done in just one day, and where your time is being spent now. You'll see how much time is actually spent productively, and how much is wasted!

- **Take five minutes** before every small task or phone call to decide what result you want to achieve. This will help you know what success looks like before you start. Then take five minutes after each task or phone call to assess whether your desired result was achieved. If not, what went wrong? How do you put it right next time?

- **Don't answer the phone** just because it's ringing, or e-mails just because they appear in your inbox. Don't instantly give people your attention unless it's absolutely crucial in your business to offer an immediate response. Instead, schedule a time to answer emails and return phone calls.

- 📧 **Avoid Facebook, Twitter** and other social media unless you use these tools to generate business.

- 📧 **Remember:** it's impossible to get everything done. Just do your best!

SAY WHAT?

> **❝** *I think it's very important whatever you're trying to make or sell... has to be good. A bad product and you know what? You won't be here in ten years.* **❞**
>
> **Martha Stewart,**
> **multimillionaire US businesswoman**

✳ Staying motivated

You're bound to face ups and downs in your new business, and one of the biggest challenges you'll face will be to keep a smile on your face when times get tough. Here's a checklist of ideas to keep you motivated:

Set yourself realistic targets — and revisit them regularly.

Think positively — congratulate yourself on things you achieve.

Make time for friends and family — strong relationships can support your success.

Have some time off — you will come back fresher and raring to go!

Visualise success — think in terms of what you will achieve, rather than the problems that might stand in your way.

GET REAL!

US teenager Adam Horwitz launched an online game called Mobile Monopoly that earned $1.5m (£950,000) in just three days! Adam, 18, puts his success down to perseverance and hard work:

"I've failed at least 30 times with different websites and stuff. But if I hadn't failed all of those times, I wouldn't be where I am now."

mobilesmonopoly.com

✳ MAINTAINING QUALITY AND SERVICE

Any small business owner will tell you that it's virtually impossible to turn down work. Fifty fairy cakes by Saturday, no problem! You might find it hard to say no, but think carefully about each new job before you accept it. Because if you miss an important deadline — birthday cakes for a party, for example — or deliver work that is not up to your usual standard, the reputation of your business will suffer, and you may end up losing work as a result.

✳ Be honest

The best idea is to be honest with yourself and with customers. If you're not confident that you can do your best work in the time scale required, either don't take it on, or be clear with the customer about your existing workload. Being honest doesn't mean the work will necessarily go elsewhere. A customer may decide to be more flexible and give you longer to do the work properly. A final piece of advice here: if the opposite happens and you find yourself with no other jobs on, never tell a customer you have no other work. Just say, 'I can fit you in'!

57

* Estimate your time

If you're going to be working hard, and producing great results, you also need to be paid fairly for the work you do. A common problem with new businesses is underestimating how long a job will take, and therefore undercharging. If you spend a full weekend baking cookies for the local coffee shop instead of the three hours you anticipated, that £20 fee doesn't seem quite as tempting! It's always easy to think that a job will be finished quicker than it really will be. If in doubt, add on some extra time and charge accordingly. Don't be nervous asking for a slightly higher fee. Customers are often prepared to pay a little more for the confidence that a job will be done properly and on time.

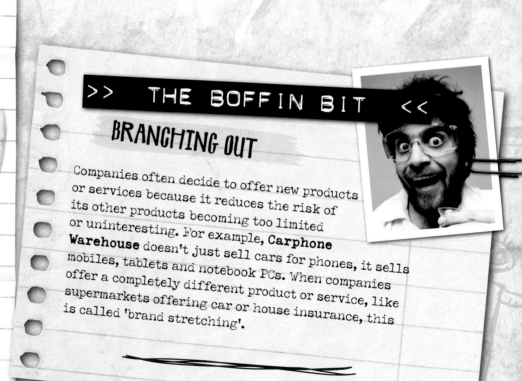

>> THE BOFFIN BIT <<

BRANCHING OUT

Companies often decide to offer new products or services because it reduces the risk of its other products becoming too limited or uninteresting. For example, **Carphone Warehouse** doesn't just sell cars for phones, it sells mobiles, tablets and notebook PCs. When companies offer a completely different product or service, like supermarkets offering car or house insurance, this is called 'brand stretching'.

Negotiate a fair price

When it comes to price, customers will often ask very early, 'How much will you charge?' Try to throw the question back at them by asking what their budget is, and how long they expect the job to take. Be flexible — you don't want to lose the work by haggling over fees, but you do want a decent rate for the work you do. Ask as many questions as you need to get a good idea of what is required before agreeing on a price and time scale.

And finally...

Enjoy it! You've planned carefully and worked extremely hard to make your business a success. Be proud of yourself. You deserve it!

BE A QUICK EXPERT!

Staying on top of a growing workload takes planning:

- Try to plan your time and don't let distractions get in the way. Not all emails need answering straight away!

- Remember your successes, and learn from your mistakes. Every mistake is a chance to improve.

- There are only 24 hours in every day. Don't take on more work than you can handle.

SWOT ANALYSIS (Strengths, Weaknesses, Opportunities and Threats)

>>>> STRENGTHS <<<<

Questions:

- Does your business do something unique?

- Is there anything innovative about it?

- What are its USPs (unique selling points)?

- Why will people use your product or service instead of a competing product or service?

It's the only eco-friendly taxi service with a disco beat. We play the passenger's requests (as long as we have the MP3) and transport them to their destination by pedal power.

Customers can sit back and enjoy the ride, listening to their favourite tunes. The rickshaw is even equipped with disco lights.

It's green (pedal power not a car), it's cheap and it's musical!

To my knowledge, there are no other services like this.

>>>>> WEAKNESSES <<<<

Questions:

- Why wouldn't people use your product or service?

- Does your business do everything it says it can do?

- Is it available to everyone?

- Is it as good or better than other similar businesses already open?

- Do you have enough manpower to cope with demand when you launch?

Bad for going long distances – or up hills.

Maximum of two passengers at a time, and limited space for luggage.

Everyone can use it – unless they are very heavy!

There are other rickshaw services, but nothing for the music-loving rickshaw passenger.

Currently only one rickshaw, so there is a limit to how many passengers can be carried in one day.

The boxes below will help you assess your business idea. We have come up with our own company and filled in the analysis to give you an idea of how it works.

Name of the business: Roland's Disco Rickshaws

>>> OPPORTUNITIES <<<

Questions:

- Can the product or service be improved in the future, eg more features added?

- Will new markets emerge for this business?

- Can the business target new 'niche' (ie small, specific) markets?

- Can it develop new USPs?

More rickshaws can be added to the fleet – if I can get friends interested in working for me.

MP3 collection will grow, and therefore larger selection of music will be offered.

We could target people going to or from discos – who don't want the music to end!

We could maybe add a tv with music channels to the rickshaw?

>>>> THREATS <<<<

Questions:

- Is the market for your product or service shrinking?

- Will new technology make your business unnecessary?

- Are any of your weaknesses so bad they might affect your business in the long run?

Cars are getting greener, so there may be less demand for pedal power.

Unless we can expand beyond one rickshaw, the business can never grow.

A larger company with more money could steal the idea and put out a whole fleet of disco rickshaws, cornering the market.

Anticipate – expect or predict

Bookkeeping – keeping financial records of a business

Crucial – extremely important; critical

Customer-centric – focussed on the needs of the customer

Deadline – the latest time or date that something has to be finished or delivered by

Drastically – extremely

Emerge – to become better known, more important or more obvious

Enhancing – increasing or improving the quality or value of something

Expanding – becoming larger or more extensive

Expenses – money spent on a product (for example ingredients or marketing)

Global market – possible customers all over the world

Guaranteed – promised with certainty

Haggling – arguing for a long time about the cost of something

Initiative – the ability to think and act by yourself, without following instructions

Innovative – introducing new ideas; advanced; original

Inquisitive – having an interest in learning things; curious

Mogul – an important or powerful person (in business)

Net income – the amount of money a business has made, taking into account the revenue and expenses

Niche market – a specialised but profitable section of the market

Organic – produced without chemical fertilizers or pesticides

Persistent – continuing to do something despite difficulties

Potential – possible

Prestigious – admired, or having a high status

Revenue – money made when selling a product or service; this amount does not take expenses into account

Spreadsheet — a computer program used for accounting, in which figures are arranged in rows and columns and can be used in calculations

Thoroughly — greatly; very much

Thrive — to prosper; grow; flourish

Trial and error — experimenting with methods of doing something to find the most successful

Vintage — something old that is high quality